# PETALS
### and thorns

# PETALS
## and thorns

### vuyisile rodolo

foreword by dr tsietsi jacob medupe

Copyright © 2023 by Vuyisile Rodolo
www.vuyisilerodolo.com

All rights reserved. This book or any portion thereof may not be reproduced or used in any manner whatsoever without the express written permission of the author or publisher, except for the use of brief quotations in a book review.

Project Manager: Fred van der Linde
Design and Layout: Ronel Niemand
Cover Design: Debbie Boettcher
Editor: Melinda Harper
Illustrator: Ifrah Fatima

Printed in South Africa
First Print 2023

ISBN: 978-0-6397-5315-7

WoodRock Publishing
South Africa
www.woodrockpublishing.com

*to my wife sibongile, and children
sibusiso, nosipho and luthando*

# *foreword*

Vuysile Rodolo's *Petals and Thorns* is a pervasive work of poetry that invites readers on an emotional journey of spiritual reflection through the revelation of secret pearls of wisdom.

Composed of several themes which mirror human emotion and experience, this work encourages readers to engage in self-reflection and wonder. Some particularly poignant themes I caught during my first reading of this work were, Belonging, Adieu, and Becoming.

It is clear that Rodolo's expression of Belonging is rooted in the idea that belonging is finding the full freedom to find and express yourself within your group of peers. This is made simpler when one discovers their strengths and weaknesses, their achievements and failings— their petals and their thorns. It is only then that the community is able to create a cohesive society in which each individual has a role to play and each individual truly belongs. When one's individual role is recognized and applied to the community, the community can then begin to work as a unit, complementing the strengths and weaknesses of one another, to create truly wonderful things.

This sense of Belonging, however, can become a double-edged sword. When one arrives at a true sense of belonging, no matter how tightly knit the community may be, one must inevitably depart. Rodolo captures this sentiment well through a meditation on one of the most painful words in human language—Adieu. This resolute and final farewell is always heart breaking, particularly when it is bid to a person one holds dear. It is, therefore, essential that friendship and love is celebrated while life still allows it. Celebrations of each other can help build the emotional strength and mental fortitude that help provide the encouragement that is needed to continue in time of turmoil and distress.

The concept of Becoming is one that is more personalised to the individual. Whether one's goal is to become more courageous, happy, or content, in order to achieve this goal, one must go through the process of self–reflection. This means that one must face themselves.

Self-discovery is the thing mankind fears the most. He is not easily offended when faced with a truth that is fully acknowledged, nor is he bothered by a blatant, bald-faced lie. Instead, he becomes sensitive or self-conscious when presented with a fact he refuses to recognize. Total self-acceptance ensures that one does not allow the successes or failures to point to a deficiency in themselves. They know that the achievements of others are based on their own hard work, rather than the failures of others. Becoming is the highest order of self-acceptance, guaranteeing an optimum maximisation of one's natural abilities. It's all in the Becoming.

These concepts of Belonging, Adieu, and Becoming allow one to begin to live their life to the fullest, knowing that living for today affects the outcome of tomorrow. The future is not something that needs to be worried about, but must be prepared for and it is taken care of, shaped, moulded, and coloured by the activities of the present. The world of today is characterised by the choices of yesterday; thus tomorrow is produced by the labours of today. Living a good life is simply a product of luck and this is made more wonderful when it is understood that luck occurs when preparedness and opportunity meet; and opportunity is and ever will be present.

The making of the good life is, however, not always easy. In fact, it rarely ever is easy. Most often, the curation of the good life is marked by repeated failures. The ultimate failure, however, is when one ceases trying out of a fear of failure. That being said, one of the greatest accomplishments of mankind has been the use of failure as a propellant to new and greater heights. With every trial, one gets closer to their goal and, after figuring out where not to go, figure out where to go.

Petals and Thorns is a meditation on the experiences of life through poetic expression that draws readers in and compels them to imagine. Rodolo, in the words of Barbara Frederickson, asks readers to begin to dream with him.

*Now imagine you are this flower, and your petals are drawn tightly around your face. If you can see out at all, it's just a little speck. You can't appreciate much of what goes on around you...But once you feel the warmth of the sun, things begin to change, your leaves begin to soften, your petals loosen and begin to stretch outward, exposing your face. And removing your delicate blinders, you see more and more and your world quite literally expands.*[1]

The presence of thorns symbolises pain. Just as there is relief after the thorn has been removed, one becomes stronger after times of distress.

Vuysile Rodolo has written quite a compelling book loaded with the beautiful characterisation of what life entails, how one becomes a victor after a life of thorns, and the strengthening experience of rest and happiness of the petals throughout the poem's language.

I hope you enjoy the work as much as I did from beginning to end.

- Dr. Tsietsi Jacob Medupe

Content Advisor: Portfolio Committee on Communications and Digital Technologies - Parliament of The Republic of South Africa

---

1   Hedges, Chris. *Empire of Illusion: The End of Literacy and the Triumph of Spectacle.* (New York, NY: Nation Books, 2009) 126

## contents

| | |
|---|---|
| **introduction** | 2 |
| **i belong** | **5** |
|    i am worthy | 6 |
|    at the right place at the right time | 11 |
|    smile | 16 |
| **pensive** | **22** |
|    adieu | 23 |
|    was i late | 30 |
|    from a distance | 39 |
|    seeking | 46 |
|    death or is it life | 53 |
|    until then | 60 |
| **i'm alive** | **65** |
|    today | 66 |
|    rhythm of my soul | 72 |
|    becoming | 78 |

## keeping the home fires burning — 90
    days like these — 91
    don't stop — 96
    onward — 98
    i've got to make it — 103

## i am — 108
    side by side — 109
    possible impossible — 118
    past present and tomorrow — 120
    by design — 124

## coda — 130
    petals and thorns — 132
    this world is beautiful — 137

## *about the author* — 145
## *acknowledgements* — 147

## *introduction*

by default, you belong to the universe

life's hurt and disappointments

don't make you unworthy

they call on you to find your voice

to be able to navigate this complex terrain


finding your voice invites you

to collaborate with yourself

to talk to and with yourself

to say the very things which make you unique

let the vibrations of your inner voice

bring to life every being that's inside you

no time to listen to the voice of modesty,

the voice of conformity


is this not the very same voice

that dries out the juices you need

to inspire you to mastery

be the master of your inner collaboration

so you can meaningfully collaborate with others

from the vantage point of authenticity


at the same time be kind to yourself

treat each life with kindness, respect

and contribute to their prosperity

find your song and master your dance

to be attuned to this beautiful world.

petals and thorns

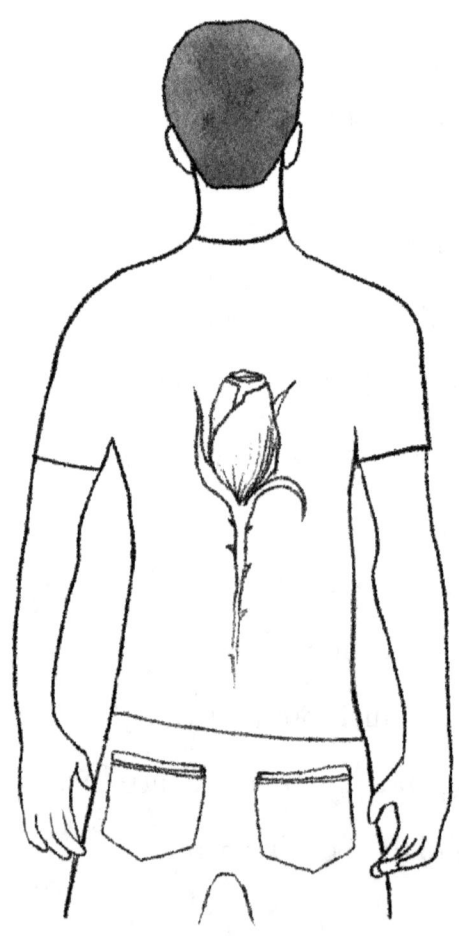

# i belong

i am one with the universe
as it is one with me
and, touching it, i am touched by it
in this oneness, i become.
in this oneness, i belong.

# i am worthy

i am born of the son of the soil,

i am born of the daughter of the universe.

from this union, i was created to be no one else but me.

from the top of my head to the depths of my soul,

i am complete, i am worthy.

how i look, when i walk,
how i talk, when i'm silent,
how i sing, when i cry,
i am, who i am.
in my perfections and imperfections, i am worthy.

i am not made up of what i own,
my failures or achievements.
my worth is not in friend nor foe,
but in the fibre of my bones
and the depths of my soul.

just like all that dwell in it

the universe is my abode.

i am not greater or lesser than another.

for in the greater scheme of creation, each has their own worth.

i am what i am, i am here because i am worthy

i show up for myself and for the universe

i strive, i live, i walk tall

i fall, i rise, i soar

in the wholeness of the universe,

i was born to thrive because,

my maker made me worthy.

# at the right place at the right time

i'm at the right place at the right time,
i can feel it within me.
i'm meant to be in this time and place.
i'm as ready for this moment as ready can be.

everything i need, i possess within me.

i can feel the inspiration

waiting to strike, to flood my veins.

with all the knowledge i need,

sitting in my mind and soul,

waiting for expression,

i am prepared.

my time has come.

the heavens smile at this time and place,
i can see the illumination of the heavens.
everything is clear as clear can be.
the heavens' genius is here within me.

i have received the genius of the heavens,
i have received guidance from the angels,
i have been prepared for this moment.
the angels of heaven and earth collaborated
to prepare me for this very moment.

i am ready to apply my knowledge,
i am prepared to apply my understanding.
i'm at the right place at the right time,
ready as ready can be.

vuyisile rodolo

# smile

worry no more, child

i'll always be by your side.

worry no more, child

for your beauty will always shine.

vuyisile rodolo

yesterday, it was einstein and newton
who engraved their names
on the everlasting scrolls of history.
today, your impact on creation will be like no other.
tomorrow, you'll live forever.

share the wealth you have in your mind.

share the worth that, in your soul, placidly abides.

with your smile, allow the world to ponder,

for today is your time.

da vinci gave the world a mona lisa smile,
chopin gave the world a smile of their own,
today your smile will warm the blossoms of love,
allowing your melody to ring forever.

today, the glow of your smile
will share with the world the beauty and warmth
which cuddle on the bosom of your soul.
an endearing masterpiece,
never seen nor experienced.
let your smile illuminate all the treasures within.

dare not cast doubt

on the gifts that lie inside you.

big or small they are gifts from god.

smile, he'll multiply them a thousand-fold.

# pensive

when the rose thorns grow,
the deeper the pigment of their petals,
when thorns prick,
the sweeter the petals' fragrance.
in one breath, i embrace the gifts of life,
whether they are the gifts of tears or joys.
through it all, i stay alive.

# adieu

what pain is this i feel?

what is this piercing inflicted in the depths of my heart?

the tearless wail strikes like lightning

on my already broken spirit.

what news is this?

my friend, the gentle giant,

the giant is no more.

my mind frantically turns back the hands of time,

recalling every moment with crystal clarity.

the laughs and the cries,

the dreams that saw no end.

yesterday, we had all the time

today, time came to an unceremonious stop.

do i mourn for him or do i sing his praises?

how do you remember the gentle giant?

how, indeed, when his memory fills your mind

in a magnitude beyond measure?

when his memory fills your heart with a smiling cry?

how do you remember him when his memory makes you wonder with awe?

do you remember him or do you mourn him?

do you mourn him or sing his praises?

do you praise him or be overcome with grief?

do you grieve the loss of him

or celebrate the goodness of the life he had?

what would he have said about himself
if he was standing here?
will he tell us about the journey after death,
his passing into old or the new jerusalem?
will he tell us about his dream to be in his father's house?

maybe, just maybe he would say,

"i loved you, i lived for you,

and now i am done with this world."

maybe he will say,

"let me go"

maybe, just maybe he will say,

"the angels have welcomed me.

i have arrived at the beginning of eternal life."

maybe he will say,

"accept that i am held

in the warm embrace of my creator."

# was i late

drip, drop, drip, drop
i can hear the weight of my tears
adding weight to my already heavy heart.
the pool of my tears rises like a tide,
weighing heavily on my unfettered spirit,
choking my throat dry.

time has passed,
turning seconds into hours,
into days and years.
decades turning, piercing, gashing,
ruining a memory that never was.

hope kept the memory thinly veiled,

though never experienced alive.

dusk turns to dawn as another day comes.

the feelings become more dense.

today is the day,

the day of unimaginable bittersweet reveal.

i allow another one pass me by,

and the elusive memory thinly weaves into dusk.

vuyisile rodolo

why did i take so long?

i ask,

will the rose bush still bless me with its fragrance,

or will its tiny thorns bring forth

the decay of time and the gruesomeness of life?

i wonder.

i should have come sooner.

i could have come earlier.

when it was young and fresh,

it could enjoy my nurturing.

yet hope speaks still more clearly.

tomorrow is another day.

today is the day.
life abounds, and the rose still to be seen.


yes, today is the day,
in joy or pain,
in sadness or delight.
petals or thorns.

deep in my soul,

from the marrow of my bones, i know.

today is the first day in all my days

i get to live.

i live the memory of a time long ago.

i feel,

my arm muscles twitch,

my fingers tremble.

the river flowing not far from the rose

seems to have found a bed within my eyes.

close, very close,

everything within me now rises with the tide.

to the garden that bore the rose i say,

i am sorry.

my heart sinks below the weight

of crushing emotions as the long day closes.

it's been too long.

i was late, the rose is gone.

how i wish the rose was still alive.

the memory that never was

and never will it be.

the rose is no more.

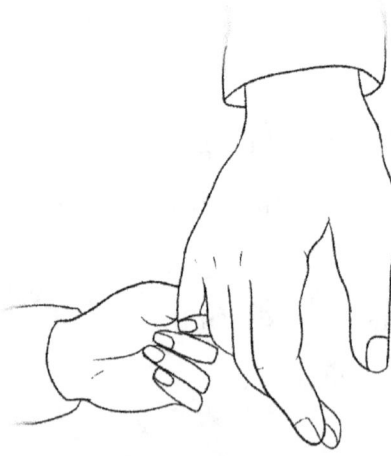

# from a distance

behold the beauty beyond compare

beauty unfathomable

beauty never experienced

a rose garden regrets its existence in your presence.

perfectly created

as if never was born and never will die

picture perfect, nothing in this life compares

only rivalled by the greek gods.

*vuyisile rodolo*

looking so pure

so delicate

so divine

that coming close to you will spoil

the pureness which only angels can contest.

pure work of art you are

the envy of leonardo da vinci

the inspiration of unending nocturnes

of poems that evoke heaven on earth.

you are endearing
but only from a distance
i should have measured the distance
to keep my heart and soul to
continue to savour the beauty untold
i guess i came too close
i should have known.

i saw you go to church
i turned into a believer
little did i know that
it was the garden of gethsemane reincarnate
the beauty of the beast
how could i have known?

how could i have known that
the temple for the goddesses
will turn into a hive
or that coming so close
would sting my heart
and create an unforgettable excruciating pain?

i should have kept the distance
'cause from a distance you were adorable
from a distance i was closer to god.

# seeking

what is it that keeps my eyes open

in the brightness of day,

in the belly of the darkest night?

i search,

seeking solace in the heart of disconsolance.

looking in the mirror,

i am watched by the eyes of a hawk,

focused to ambush the unassuming prey

scatter the little birdies

looking for a place to hide.

the laser focus of the

multiplicity of public eyes on mine

pierces through the pores of my skin

searching my wanting, empty soul

their gaze feels heavy on my shrinking shoulders

and my despairing spirit

in the midst of vast array of shining stars

like an outcast, i feel.

success i see, failure i taste

like a sheep in the presence of wolves

i shrink.

vuyisile rodolo

in solitude, i tend my ego

bruised from the whipping of days gone by.

will it ever pass? i wonder.

how long will my enslavement end?

how long before my exodus from egypt come?

i ruminate.

past strikes that i suffered

supplant the knowledge that i am capable.

where is the door out of this labyrinth?

when will my respite come?

how long, how long,

how long will it last?

i have forgotten how to live,

how to be thankful.

fear has painted every blessing

with a brush of desolation.

my saviour is my knowledge that i am able,

i know i can.

i can escape this dungeon
of mental and spiritual captivity.
if i fail again, it will not take away my being.
my humanity cannot be taken by failures.

i am grateful for the gift of being worthy,
i am grateful,
for the angels that are holding out for my recovery.
i will make it.
i will overcome.

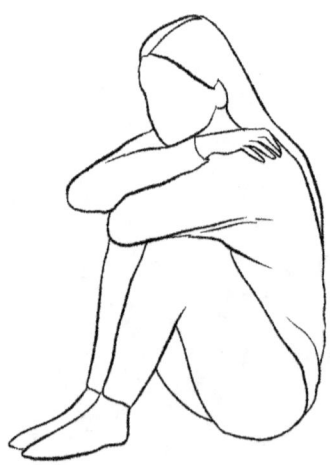

# death or is it life

tossing, turning, in a trance
tick, tock, tick, tock
the chirping chiming of the clock.
gasping breaths slip slowly through life.
lifeless dream through timeless slumber,
lifeless slumber,
this is death.

open eyes and, seeing, sightless.
senseless and unfeeling touch,
sounds and images are bright and
void of life, not giving much.
waveless, soundless ears unhearing,
make no sense of life or death.

becoming numb to your heart beating,
you lose existence of your mind.
in and out, meaningful breathing
meaningless as days go by.
and when there's no difference or sameness,
living a life of indifference,
this is lifeless, this is death.

every moment passes by,

no momentum now is gained.

limbs intact and still no movement,

aimless plodding every day.

waiting, waiting, and still waiting

will it come, whatever is best?

time passes, slowly, slowly grating,

this is lifeless, this is death.

wake up, you've waited for too long
still trapped in living death's own claws.
so while you're here and still not gone,
while living, death must heed our laws.
death has no place in the land of the living.

awaken to the light of life,
awaken in your limbs their sense.
awaken now and join the strife
and hearing now, begin to dance.
awake and live whilst you're alive,
by your example, death revive.

you are more than a sleeping body
in the grove of the awake.
you're worth more, than to embody
purposeless grinding day to day.

while you're in this world for good reason
wake up and, yourself forgiving.
know you have what this world needs and
know death has no place with the living.

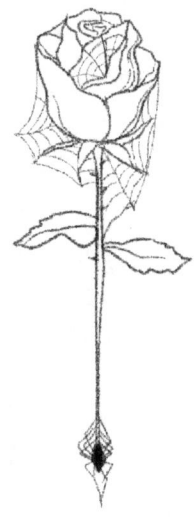

# until then

did he just say that?
when did i do that?
he says my life was one of impact.
that blows my mind.

the mood is so sombre.

the music can do with a little upbeat.

even though i was on the quieter side

i still enjoyed some beautiful grooves.

she says,

i inspired individuals to be the best they could be.

that my work tuned the chords of the human spirit to solve rather than create problems.

hmm, i'm listening,

the man above must be dancing with joy.

vuyisile rodolo

at last, the mood is more on the groovy side.
speaker after speaker orate,
about how i contributed to
them experiencing heaven on earth.
the elevation of a nation
and generations to come.
i could hear a whisper at the back,
"stop it, you can't speak ill of the dead."

what a send-off,

what a memorial.

after all what is said and done,

it looks like i got a special invitation

to join the legion on the right-hand side in heaven.

well, until then

i will live to bring this ideal to life.

# i'm alive

no matter what life throws at me
my dreams will shine like light.
i stay true to my core,
never will i fake it.
at all times i take the road to mastery,
at all times i dance to the rhythm of my soul.

## today

today is a new day.
new thoughts, new drive.
it is real, it is here.
yesterday is past and gone,
tomorrow is only an illusion.
it, too, might never come.

today is the best day of my life.

no other time is best to live than now.

it is in today that i can breathe life into my potential,

today's opportunities remain possible

when yesterday's have passed away.

today, i have a chance to bring tomorrow to life,

this day's endeavour brings tomorrow within reach

don't linger on yesterday,

live in the time you have.

if yesterday was good, allow a smile,

let it shine brightly on the possibilities of today.

if yesterday was bad,

take the lessons that it afforded you.

the lessons which make today even greater,

don't live in the past of yesterday

life happens one day at a time,
today i celebrate that i am alive.
tomorrow is only a dream,
allow yourself to make tomorrow's dream real
by the choices you make today.
don't live in the illusion of tomorrow.

today is my day.
i use today's energy to create and live
the life i dream of.
it is the day that has been reserved for me.

no person, good or bad,
    will take it from me
        no memory, good or bad,
            will snatch it away
                no dream, good or bad,
                    will steal it from me.

never was a day like this,
there never will be one like it.
everything i need to do,
i do it now.
today is the best time i will ever have,
it is real, it is here.
don't let this day pass you by.

# rhythm of my soul

my life began,

one in a million to one.

solitary, in a bubble i was protected.

i kicked, as life began to find its rhythm

moment by moment, the rhythm got stronger.

i turned, i kicked, i broke.

i cried, from one to millions.

vuyisile rodolo

a different rhythm i found in the world of millions,
a different rhythm i learnt from the tens.
the ten grew to thousands
and the beat of the rhythm changed.
no one told me the rhythm would change.
i adapted, i learnt the different rhythms of the soil.

the soil wanted me to master its rhythm,

how can i, when there's so much dissonance?

survival of the fittest, eat or be eaten,

believe or be broken,

the law of the soil.

how can the child of the soil master the rhythm

when there's so much emptiness and brokenness.

not until i appreciate the rhythm within
will i truly master the rhythm without.
not until the rhythm within is in tune with itself
will i truly appreciate the rhythm without.
not until i breakout from the bubble of the millions
will i find the voice of my own rhythm.

minim by minim, the rhythm of one grows stronger,
beat by beat, the drums within gets in tune,
minute by minute the rhythm within
attunes with the galaxy of stars above.
strand by strand, every muscle fibre gets
stronger and stronger,
ready to dance,
dance to the rhythm of my soul,
dance with the rhythm of the soil.

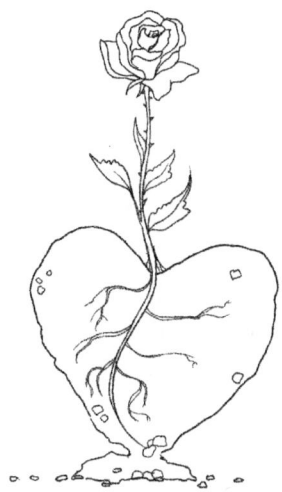

from the liberation of the rhythm of my soul
i have found the key to modulate the cadences.
this is the day,
i dance to the tune
from within the depths of my soul.
today my soul finds the rhythm
of yesterday, today, and tomorrow.
from within, i truly enjoy the dance from without.
i am the master of the rhythm of my soul.

# becoming

i am awake, i am alive.

my senses are enlivened

to the world around me.

i am awake to the life of another day.

without fail, the sun rises,
the splendour of the day strolls into my life.
the sun shines on me again.
i am the most blessed person in the world,
to hear the birds of the morn
singing their happy tune.
reminding me
this is a new dawn, a new day, a new chance to be me.
without fail, i get another chance to create who i am.

the rising sun brings life
to all that lay asleep.
i can smell the dews as the grass
awakens from its slumber.
i can smell the flowers' fragrance,
and see their vibrant colours.
the grasses, the trees,
they all beckon me to take part in creation,
in making this, the best day ever lived.

vuyisile rodolo

how can i be otherwise,
when all of nature wakes up with a smile,
greeting a new day
full of possibilities?
the bright sun shines vividly on them,
i can touch them, i can taste them
i can feel myself immersed in them.

today, i am alive to only one,

that is, the one i am going to create.

just like nature unreservedly gave

a beautiful sweet morning just to me,

i am using all my faculties to create the best of me.

i owe it to my guide, to nature,

i dare not let this beautiful day go to waste.

each second that ticks by brings my efforts to life.

each minute that passes brings shape to my sweat.

each hour that strikes locks in the creation of my endeavours.

in each moment, i become the person i want to be.

each moment of today i am living in the creation of myself.

the rain drops make dew on the grass.
just like the dew feeds the grass,
i am fortified by the rain.
but when the storm begins,
it feels like the beautiful day will never be again.

i am alive to the resilience of nature.
though clouds may cover,
the sun never fails to shine,
the grass and the trees are rejuvenated.
i choose to accept the resilience of nature.
after every thunderstorm of life,
i rise renewed and stronger.

oh, the golden radiance of the sunset
retreats, smiling, at today's work well done.
as the day closes, i take stock at what i have done,
big or small,
    easy or challenging,
        good or bad,
            smiles or tears.

i celebrate everything i've done to create today,
i celebrate all the guidance i received
on how to become the better version of myself.
i celebrate just a chance to be alive,
i celebrate the creation of another great memory.

the moon rises,

the night cometh,

time to rest

and allow the fruits of today's labour to grow

at night, the stars gently glimmer in the sky,

i allow the them to softly shine over my soul,

to offer dreams and refresh me for another day.

in my dreams, my senses are enlivened to my new life.

in my dreams, i am alive to me

who is becoming.

vuyisile rodolo

# keeping the home fires burning

no matter where life takes me,
i'll be there with it.
when life happens, i will happen with it.
i am exquisite, i am worthy,
i am complete.
i am anointed to be the best of me.

# days like these

the light shines on me,
the rays of the sun form a halo around me.
the energy of the light fortified me as it shines.
i am great, i am invincible.
it is days like these that makes me believe.

challenge after challenge,

i stand and deliver.

hurdle after hurdle,

i prevail.

days like these, reminds me how blessed i am.

from the dusty streets of the hood,

from the grind and the drudgery of township survival,

i rose to the challenges,

i conquered.

days like these come and the memory lives on.

the love lost makes way for love gained.

disappointment of the moment,

hurt that lasts but for a time,

feeds the field of a deep and everlasting love.

the momentum of days like these keeps the hope.

every time i see the light
at the end of a long dark tunnel,
every time i gain strength
after being battered by life's tragedies,
every time i spring back after a setback,
i know that i am protected and honoured
by the guidance of the omnipotent.
days like these enable me to say,
"it, too, will pass."

# don't stop

taking it step by step
moving decisively towards your goal
hurdles in your way
don't stop


        dense is the nightly darkness
        thick are the clouds of day
        thinly fades tomorrow's hope
        don't stop


                bruised from the unrewarded efforts
            crushed by the unforgiving ruthlessness of failure
                  hold on to the promise of tomorrow
                              don't stop

ruffled by the harsh winds of the season
shaken by the roar of thunder
blown by the storms of the day
don't stop

           take it step by step
           bruises and scars heal
           and the sun never fails to shine again
           you dare not stop

                      follow the rainbow
                      hold on to your dreams
                      for tomorrow promises a fresh start
                      don't you ever stop

## onward

tears in my eyes,
tearing of my heart,
never will they stop my onward journey.
for therein lies the hopes and dreams
which to my mind and eyes brings.

over every trial,

every tribulation,

every setback and disappointment

i stand resolute to triumph.

no failure is unassailable,

no mountain is insurmountable,

no fear nor trepidation will paralyse

my efforts on an onward journey.

for i am a warrior

from heaven and earth
cometh the light that guides my spirit.
in every step of my peregrination,
both the lights within and out,
illuminates my unshakable belief that
i am enough, i am complete,
i am endowed with the gifts from the almighty
and those who've been before me.

i am the son of the soil.

the triumph of the heavens flow through me,

i am unstoppable, i am unshakable.

onward and forward,

every tribulation and pain shall move me.

for victor i am, victim never will i ever be.

# i've got to make it

no one but me, nobody but i.

none above, none below,

none around me.

from dawn to dusk, it is i.

the burning desire within me,
the desire which fuels every thought,
that flows through my brain
igniting all my senses along the way,
the fountain of life, ever unseen,
never understood, nor experienced.
the burning desire that breathes life
today, tomorrow and forever.

no smiling tyrant will dampen the fire that burns
from the bosom of my soul.
no sheep-like comforter will lull me
to believe everything is good.
when slowly, flame by flame,
spark by spark,
the fire within dies.
for the whispers of reason and possibility
are louder and stronger than all others.

i call on all the strands of fortitude,
the rocks of resilience,
the bulwarks of all that is the substance of life
to stand guard.
i call on all the fibres of my muscles,
the fibre of my being,
the grit which i have hard won,
to keep the home fires burning.
this burning desire is much more precious
than to let its flames die.

no one but me has been chosen for this mission,
the heavenly host whispered to none other but i.
the blessings of all of the support,
guidance, and protection
all the abilities, capabilities, gifts bestowed upon me
to master this mission.
this is my story,
    this is my song
        this is my dance,
            i will make it.

# i am

my dreams mirror life that was,
a connection to life that one day will be.
they prepare me to receive the chalice
from those before me
to serve to those after me

# side by side

darkness and light,

feminine and masculine,

heavenly and worldly,

life and death,

day in, day out, we live in their eternal presence,

it is neither good nor bad,

nor right, nor wrong,

neither black nor white.

in the brightness of day

and the darkness of the night,

they all dwell together

in the continuum of relativity.

nature evolves in the passing of seasons,
the winter's good gives way to summer's greatness.
nocturnal and diurnal all living together
 in their space and time.
side by side, all nature
lives, feeds, thrives.

can or cannot,

possible or impossible,

belief or disbelief,

live in the presence of each other.

in one, there is the other.

it all depends.

it all depends on what we know or don't,
on what we have experienced or have not,
on what we choose to believe or not to.

the truth of the 21$^{st}$ century
is truly different from that of the 16$^{th}$
how do i know that what i hold as absolute truth today
could turn out to be relative through the ages?
for now, it is good enough.
it makes my world go round.

through failures, i have learnt to embrace success,
through sadness, joy i cherish.
as each gives way to another,
as the sun and the moon share the universe,
as the evolution of nature reveals
the indefiniteness of definition,
i am awake to the knowledge that
what seem impossible for me today,
creates everlasting possibilities.
the revelation is just the beginning.

the beginning of a new life,
the beginning of a new self,
the appreciation of the light and the dark in me,
the realisation of the titan within,
the rise from the ashes of pain and strain,
yes, the revelation is just the beginning.

how could i not see it?
when mother nature spells it out
day in, day out.
that the understanding of life's antithesis
is the source of living.
the winters of life are the very creators
of fresh, healthy and strong beginnings.
that the dark days of life incubates renewal and growth
oh, but it is just the beginning.

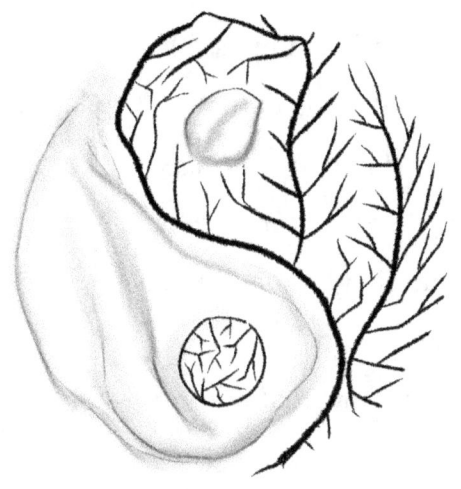

how could it be that i did not realise
that every time i rise from the fall
i create better days of my life?
the tireless strengthening of the fibres of resilience
hails the greater days of my life.
indeed,
the revelation is only the beginning.

# possible impossible

possible, impossible
what is the difference?
doing, not doing,
being, not being
could that be the difference?

how do i know that it is impossible
until i do it?
how do i know i am capable
of making the impossible possible?
i won't know,
unless i do it.

could impossible be spelling
the state of being possible?
could impossible be spelling i am capable?
could it be spelling the choice to be?

i believe i am, i believe i can,
i believe,
i'm endowed with abundant capabilities,
that the desire within is greater
than the hurdles without
therefore, i do.

i choose to do,
i choose to be,
i choose to make the impossible
possible

## past present and tomorrow

in the beginning,

the universe opened

and gave abode to man.

one with it, she fed and sheltered.

one with it she learnt how to be.

one with the universe, man created what came to be.

i am a descendant of the wise men of the past.

i bear the wisdom to those who come after.

i am the vessel, the curator, the steward

of the wisdom of the giants

who graced and blessed the earth that feeds me.

i carry the torch of the ancient protectors,
i am fed from the spiritual giants of the ages,
i sip from the bottomless cup
filled by those philosophers
from centuries gone by.
i shelter in the comfort of creation
of the body and soul of man
who dared to live whilst they were alive

i carry the spear of the warriors of yesterday,
the defenders of true life.
i sharpen the spear that pierces
through the veil of ignorance and disdain.
i live whilst i'm alive
to give life to the warriors of tomorrow.

vuyisile rodolo

# by design

i come from the breed that knows

how to prevail over strife

i come from them that tasted hunger

and found strength to overcome

from those who walked the path

interlaced with possibilities and favour

through scorns and derision, they pressed on
to make better their lot and those after them
through it all they learnt how to become
it is not by accident that i am
i am by design

through centuries of life and living

the design was crafted within

footprints of striving and thriving weaves my dna

it has created the greatness in me

to that i am grateful

i am grateful to the heavens

for creating circumstances

providing protection and guidance

to overcome

to conquer along the way

by nature, to carry on the craft

laying fertile ground for the me that's becoming

for those who will be after i've been

it is not a fluke of nature that i am
it is nature's design that i've been
and am becoming

there are times i labour under the spell of rumination
gazing at the stars
reminding me that i am a work of art

i am the collaboration of those who have been

those who are

those who will be

heavenly grace has allowed me to become

i am me by design and the craft continues

i am by design

the design that is me thrives on

# coda

in pain and strife,
i'll be the beacon of light
in triumph and joy,
i will be the host
my presence is common to all life.
the quality of my presence affects their quality of life
through it all, i am the warrior,
i am the conqueror.

vuyisile rodolo

# petals and thorns

thorns lay beneath pools of colour and fragrance

petals, covering the ground like velvet

beaconing the love-stricken pair to the bosom of the other

colour, which fills the soul with tenderness and courage

you get used to the prick

you begin to appreciate the value of pain

the beautiful colours and fragrances of my garden
hide the thorns that supports and protect them
they shadow the toiling which brought them to life
seasonal and perennial species all grace my garden
i choose which one to painstakingly
lovingly tend to colourful blossom
with a little help from the heavenly grace

such is life

full of colour and splendour

beaconing you to live life abundant

whose true enjoyments lie beneath

the toils and troubles of the day

without work, there is no reward

so, get use to the prick

enjoy the journey

life is a big party
put it right you enjoy it greatly
glasses and chairs may break
but the cheers and dance go on
every palate dazzled to the divinely curated table
cheers to the chef

the floor is alive with the

left and right footed all joining in the dance

enjoying the party

it's alive, it's life

live it on

raise them high to the host.

# this world is beautiful

the break of dawn

the opening of the view to

the soul of the universe

a glimpse of life to be

a window to this world beautiful

a breeze, my skin awakes

sunrise

the beauty of the meeting

of the eyes of the sky

one closes the other opens

the opening of the rays

the warmth of break of day

greets the beautiful smiles of the universe

vuyisile rodolo

steps of the hood
stomps of the hoofs
whispers of the fens
celebrates the beauty of life
the maker gave us all

the whistle of birds

makes sweet music in the blue sky

the clicks and grunts of schools of fish

echo in the deep blue ocean

high in the blue, deep in the blue

beauty abounds

vuyisile rodolo

the landscapes of this world
rise and fall across its face
standing in honour
the snowy white mountain peaks
with its green throughs
form a crown jewel to the beauty of creation

oh me, oh my

this world is beautiful

the golden heart of the sun

in its glorious splendour

glows on the horizon

unifying the deep blue seas

with the deep blue skies

the smiling moon rises in glory,
bidding adieu to the retiring sun
in its grandeur, the moon welcomes
the galaxy of shining stars
sparkling and twinkling over the nocturnal;
they too have their turn to savour the undisturbed beauty
this world is beautiful
and, with mankind as the crown of creation
it is more beautiful with me in it.

# about the author

Vuyisile Rodolo is a finance business partner and a teacher.

Most of all as a coach and a leader, his students are independent thinkers who collaborate not conform. As a result, they contribute to making this world more beautiful by bringing out the best in other people.

It is his sincere belief that you have a right and an obligation to become the best version of yourself as you dream, learn, do, unlearn, relearn, do and repeat to eternity.

# acknowledgements

To all my teachers, good and bad, from whom I have learnt how to live whilst I am alive.

To Mindvalley and Evercoach for introducing me to some of the best inspirational teachers in the world. Without this platform I might not have received inspiration from head coach Ajit Nawalkha. Yes, Ajit, I will always be a work of art.

To my inspirational fountain: thank you, Lisa Nichols, for making me realise that no one can do me better than me. Thanks for the message that I do not need permission to do me.

Dr John Demartini, from you I learnt that in me I have all that I need to be the best of me.

Thank you, Janne Robinson, for your message, "it is selfish to keep your gift to yourself", which gave me the final push to publish this book.

Thank you, all my students, past and present. Through you I have learnt how to use my voice for impact and be a life-long learner. Thanks to my coaching students for allowing me to co-create your leadership journey.

Thank you to my publishing team at WoodRock Publishing, the editor, Melinda Harper and illustrator, Ifrah Fatima.

Thank you for reading this book. I hope you found inspiration, from the thoughts written on the pages before this, to make each day better than the one before. You are worthy of being the best person you possibly can be.

www.ingramcontent.com/pod-product-compliance
Lightning Source LLC
Chambersburg PA
CBHW072006290426
44109CB00018B/2151